ROHTASGARH FORT

ROHTASGARH FORT

Wopendranath Ghosh, B.A.
(Bengal Provincial Civil Service)

PRABHAT
PRAKASHAN

Published by
PRABHAT PRAKASHAN PVT. LTD.
4/19 Asaf Ali Road,
New Delhi-110 002 (INDIA)
e-mail: prabhatbooks@gmail.com

ISBN 978-93-5186-975-7
ROHTASGARH FORT
by Shri Wopendranath Ghosh, B.A.

Edition
2025

Price
₹ 200.00 (Rupees Two Hundred only)

Printed at
R-Tech Offset Printers, Delhi

Preface

As early as 1884-86, I received great encouragement from the late Sir William Hunter, in making researches into the past history of ancient places and I had the honour and pleasure to furnish that great and earnest Student of Indian History, with the results of my humble researches. The conditions and circumstances of the public service to which I belong have indeed left little leisure for pursuing with adequate ardour and earnestness, the many interesting subjects of inquiry which the stations in which I was posted presented. I had to confine my spare moments with official literary work, such as the preparation of manuals, returns and notes on official matters. Bearing however in mind the kind words of encouragement of "Sir, William Hunter and of my father, late Balm Sree Nath Ghose, who was a collaborator in the field of education in Calcutta with the memorable David Hare since 1835, I have always endeavoured to know and learn the past history of notable places with which I came in contact in the course of my service."

During my tenure of service in the district of Shahabad many places of historical interest came to my notice among which the hill fortress of Rohtasgarh appeals strongly to the imagination by its great antiquity. I may mention that in 1904, I read with singular attention the learned speech of Lord Curzon, then Viceroy and Governor-General of India, to pass an Act to provide for the preservation of ancient monuments and of objects of archaeological, historical or artistic interests. It increased my desire for researches. I visited the Rohtas Hill fortress only before my transfer from the district in 1906. The materials collected over two years ago, I had very few moments at my disposal to put together to form a connected tale, because of the onerous duties devolved on me in connection with Two Canal Revenue Divisions in lower Bengal being amalgamated and placed under my charge.

I have annexed four sheets of lithographic plans to illustrate the places of interest which invite the visitor's attention on the Hill. My thanks are due to Pundit Harihor Bandopadhaya, of Narsrigunj who gave me the names of the kings of the solar line from the Bhagavad Gita and to

Moulvi Anis-uz-zaman Khan M.A.B.L. who translated into English the Persian inscriptions. I shall be thankful if the paper which I have composed will attract the notice of abler students of ancient India with sufficient leisure and opportunities for further research.

—Wopendranath Ghosh

Cuttack,
March 1908

Preface to Reprint Edition

Esteemed as one of the oldest (ancient) regions of human civilisation in India, Bihar has a rich culture inherited from various dynasties and birthplace of great personalities and several religions. There are many historically and culturally important places which attracts people from all walks of life and from different regions.

The republication of the book, *Rohtasgarh,* by Wopendranath Ghosh, a member of the Bengal Provincial Civil Service in the early decades of twentieth century is an important step in the direction. The book was first published in 1908 and has its origin in author's sincere and keen interest in the past history of the notable places with which he came during contact during the course of his service.

This deeply researched book is about Rohtasgarh Fort which is an important historical and cultural site of Bihar located in present Rohtas district. It has its history connected with the ancient, medieval and modern history of Bihar. The place in ancient India is associated with the exploits of Satyavadi Raja Harishchandra who is famous for his love of truth and charity. It is believed that the place has been named after his son Rohitaswa in whose memory there has been a temple on the hills. In medieval India the Fort was well-known for its strength and invincibility and always proved a challenge to invaders. Even Shershah Suri is reported to have received the Fort from the Raja of Rohtasgarh as a gift. He is also credited to have constructed a Mosque inside the Fort. In the late eighteenth century, the Fort was handed over to the British East India Company by the then Raja Saho Mal through the Act of permanent settlement.

It is my firm belief that republication of historical works such as this one, finds a new life among the readers which otherwise would have been lost in the shelves of archives and libraries. I hope this book will enlighten the historians as well as general readers who are interested in knowing our rich cultural heritage in general and Rohtasgarh Fort in particular.

The book 'Rohtas Gargh' written by Shri Wopendranath Ghosh was given to me by Srikantjee. I have found this book very interesting, informative and useful for the study of history and culture of Bihar. If this book is republished it would not only reach to a wider audience but would also help in the preservation of this valuable piece of research work for future generations.

19-01-2015 —**Dr. Abhay Kumar**

Head Dept. of History
D.A.V. Post Graduate College
Siwan

Rohtas

In offering these pages to the reader on the Rohtas Hill Fortress in the District of Shahabad, all that I intend is to explain with what great antiquity the place is connected, and to relate what lie there worthwhile to see and the facts of history they illustrate. That there is at present no connected account of all this, is the incentive to take up the work, though I feel it might have been better done by an abler hand.

Religious

If India has now attracted the attention of the whole civilized world, it is for her ancient intellectual grandeur and her religion. The sages of the land have expounded the distinction between the real and unreal and that the divine essence is in every man. This idea is the basis of the Hindu Religion and is in agreement with Theosophy, the philosophy of Kant and Schelling's, "Oneness of subjective and objective" and that of Fichte to Hegel's, "Being and non-being are indentical." This Religion has remained unchanged, stood the test of the great philosophic movements of the past and present and formed the character of a people, unsurpassed in the ancient and modern world. The great heritage of India of modern times is found in the belief, faith and hope of the people who yet discern the touch of divinity in all around themselves, who live and die, as they believe, at His will and who suffer and enjoy by His dispensation. This ideal of ancient India, the traveller sees in the great Temple of Rohitaswa on the Rohtas Hill.

The legend which the Rohtas Temple is associated with is known to all readers of ancient Indian literature. The great faith, the greater hope, which the legend brings home to the mind of the Hindu believer of ancient and modern days, offer matter for reflection to all thinkers. Modern India is not the country which will possess in the near future an institute to assist unremunerative research. There is no Indian boy or girl who does not know the legend of Raja Harischandra and does not read and repeat it without tears in the eyes and veneration for the great faith, and love for the truth which Harischandra displayed. But yet we have not a scholar, who can devote himself to the study of the immortal tale, like Dr. Somner who produced two volumes of critical study on Sir Thomas Malory's "Morte de Arthur", warmly welcomed by all lovers of mediaeval literature in Europe. There are none among the Indian enthusiasts for the country's good to induce a scholar of ancient literature to study and localize the scene of Raja Harischandra's deeds, like the German scholar, who for his excursions into the past, to unearth the tale of Arthur and his Round Table, sought and found means in the Carnegie Institute in America, Great were the knights of the Round Table and their adventures, greater still was Raja Harischandra and his son Rohitaswa and their actions. Professor Monier Williams said in his "Indian Epic Poetry,"—"The duty of studying the past history of our Eastern Empire so far as it can be collected from the ancient Sanskrit literature can no longer be evaded by educated men."

Raja Harischandra and his son are immortal for their religious disposition—displaying faith, love of truth and charity. They were Hindus and have shown what Hinduism professed. A European Scholar of Indian Literature (Dr. G.A. Grierson) has thus said about "Hinduism" recently. "Four thousand years ago it was a joyful, lusty, nature worship; three thousand years ago it was an introspective selfish pantheism; two thousand years ago it had discovered the grace of charity but knew nought of faith and hope; and a thousand years later the two last named virtues had also been discovered, and under the indirect influence of early Christianity had led people to believe in a loving personal God who became incarnate to relieve the world of sin."—Too little has been said by the learned doctor of the great ideas which run through the course of Hinduism, in the fewest possible words. Grace of charity, faith and hope pervaded the Religion for many hundreds of centuries before the time fixed for such virtues among the Hindus, and the story of Raja Harischandra and his son is a brilliant picture of the same. In Miss Manning's "Ancient and Mediaeval India" we read, "Knowing nothing of the Hindu mind or the Hindu literature and taking it for granted that whatever was heathen must be bad, the first missionaries attempted to root up wheat and tares without discrimination. The more usual effect was that those whom the teacher desired to influence, flatly refused to listen. In an instant they shrunk into themselves. Just as, some may see, a bed of the graceful sensitive plants suddenly turn stale and stiff when touched by an idler's stick. India is in truth a sealed book to those who approach it without sympathy."

In fact a comparative study of the language of the ancient Hindu literature,—its vocabulary, grammar, diction and rhetoric alone can show that its development has been a matter of thousands of years. The religious thoughts which pervade that literature were no doubt conceived in many centuries. To discuss the hundreds of views on this religion now placed before the educated world, by scholars who have studied the subject from the extant books analytically, instead of following the chain of thoughts running through them *a posteriori* cannot be the scope of this work. The ages when the literature was produced are far off and what we have to do today is to enquire, know and conceive what existed then.

The stages of Hinduism can be more correctly counted by '*Yuga Dharma'*, than by centuries. The ancient religious literature of the Hindus assigns four *Yugas,* viz. '*Satya', '*Tret*a*', '*Dicapar*' and '*Kali*'—each based on a fresh evolution of religious thought.

In the earliest *Yuga,—Sutya Yuga,*—the priest (*Guru*) prepared his disciple by asking him "to know himself." The disciple's attention was thus drawn to his material body. Then he came to know by certain practices, (*sadhanas*) that there was something beyond the material body and he asked his preceptor, (*Guru*) what was the moving spirit in the material body. Again and again he studied and came to know that there was a mind—a *Jnan,* a sense devoid of pain and pleasure, *i.e.,* the material body was the outer cell of others viz, *Monomaya, Jnanamaya,* and *Anandmaya Kos.* The disciple then sat in his *yoga* and realized the great truth '*Soham'* i.e. I am He.

This great *sadhana* changed with the next evolution and then followed the *Treta Yuga.* Mankind was then initiated into the religion by another simpler mode. The Rishis prescribed sacrifice of powers of life before the divine power. Thus came the age of *Jagna.* They realized that, 'power in matter' evolved the idea of creator. That power was all but limited and that all powers were subordinated to His, the Creator's, all that existed merged in Him. Thus was Hindu religion taught in the second stage of its evolution.

Time advanced and then came the third stage of evolution of the religion. Mankind was found unable to conceive and realize the Creator in the way they did in *Satya* and *Treta Yugas* as absolute. They began worship of Him by symbols.

Idols were conceived to depict His powers and resources and thus what they lost in mental powers were made up by *Sradha* and *Bhakti i.e.* Faith and Veneration with which they now worshipped Him. They learnt to offer Him flowers and water, fruits and incense and thus He permeated all they could conceive. When this idea was confirmed in man, he saw all symbols live and subside in the great all-pervading consciousness and he found himself lost in it.

The fourthstage of evolution of the religion is that we live in. It is known as *Kali Yuga.* Now mankind can not move upon the track their progenitors trod. The *Guru* now taught men to follow the God-men, to know His *Abatars,* incarnations. Ramkrishna Paramhansa taught his disciples to conceive and recount *'Naham' i.e.* it is not me. Thus they forget themselves and learn to live in Him.

The assignment of period by centuries does not explain the great changes the religion underwent. The highest idea has changed gradually to the simpler mode of thought and not that its development was from the imperfect to the sublime. Ages have preceded the highest conception and ages will follow before the highest is attained again.

In the *Satya Yuga* lived Raja Harischandra. He was a scion of the solar race many generations before Ramchandra, the hero of Ramayana. The legend of Harischandra is too well-known. He was son of Raja Trisanku regarding whom the following legend is told—Raja Trisanku prayed to his *Guru* Basista for elevation to Heaven in his material body. Basista declared it as impossible. Then he went to his sons if they could help him in his desire. Irritated by the Raja's most unreasonable and proud desire, they pronounced a curse that he should be a *Chandal*. Trisanku in his unclean body, as he was called a *Chandal*, repaired to the *asrama* of Biswamitra who happened to be the opponent of Basista. Biswamitra was a *Kshatrya* Raja. Once upon a time he being astonished with the wonderful powers of Basista's *Kamdhenu* wished to possess her. Finding that the request was neglected he wanted to possess the *Kamdhenu* by force. In the conflict Biswamitra lost all he had. Then he sat upon his *yoga* for powers to fight Basista. Again defeated he began *yoga* to become a *Brahman*, which aim was fulfilled by the grace of God. Thus *Biswamitra* got groat powers with which he promised Trisanku the pleasure and honour of going to Heaven in his material body. Biswamitra directed him to celebrate *yagna* to the Gods in which the Rishis declined to join. But through fear of Biswamitra they all acceded except Basista. *Yagna* was complete, when half on his ascent, Trisanku was hurled down by the Gods in Heaven, but stayed where he was by the will of Biswamitra. The tears of Trisanku poured down and flowed as the river Karamnasha—Raja Harischandra was famous for his charity, faith and love of truth. Once he incurred the ire of Biswamitra by breaking his *yoga,* when he went to hunt in the forest where Biswamitra lived. Biswamitra was resolved to punish him. He induced him to promise to give whatever he asked. Afterwards he appeared before Harischandra when he was distributing clarity and demanded all his wordly possession. In his devotion to truth he relinquished his kingdom to the great Rishi Biswamitra in *Dan* (Charity), and again to pay *Dakshina* he saw his great wife Saibya sell herself to be a slave and parted with her and his son; when he found that money fell short of the *Dakshina,* he sold himself and lived the life of a *Chandal* in the cremation ground at Kasi. There was enacted the last of the tragic scene when the slave Queen brought the dead body of her son, Rohitaswa, for cremation. They recognized each other and found themselves face-to-face with Dharmaraj, Their love for truth, the charity and sacrifice they had made for its sake, was praised by Dharmaraj who by his touch resuscitated Rohitaswa and showered on them all the blessings man could expect.

It is this resuscitation of Rohitaswa which was commemorated by the great temple on Rohtas Hill. From this legend it is clear that in that age, man by devotion could aspire for the highest grace, that *yagna* was the means to its attainment, that charity was granted without pleasure and pain of mind and with hope and love of truth and that the scene of the legend lay in the territory from Kasi to the hills about the river Karamnasha.

Chronological

Chronology in ancient literature in India does not appear to have been the aim either for the writer or the events described. The writers devoted themselves to the results of events. This being so each epoch is marked by its character rather than by the years. This is clear enough from all old works on historical events now extant.

Dr. Buhler said that Mahabharata was not merely an epic poem but was looked upon as a *Smriti* or sacred tradition. Dr. Buhler has further shown that inscriptions of about A.D. 500 quote the Mahabharata as an authority on sacred law and describes it as a bulky work containing 100,000 verses. And as we must allow some time, say a century or two, for the gradual development of this sacred character, he concludes that the Mahabharata certainly was a *Smriti* or *Dharma Sastra* from A.D. 300 and that about A.D, 500 it did not differ essentially in size and in character from its present text. Dr. Buhler adds that further researches, "Will in all probability enable us to push back the lower limits which have been thus established by four to five centuries and perhaps even further." Boff declared that not all parts of the epic are of the same age, that many parts are later additions while others may go back to a time far anterior to the date of the composition or compilation of the poem. Goldstucker expressed the Mahabharata as a collection of literary products belonging to widely distant period. The war between the *Kurus* and the *Panchalas* forms the subject of the Mahabharata. Bentley and Archdeacon Pratt have gone over the calculation on the position of the solistial points recorded to mark the date of the Vedas, the compiler of which sacred work, was a contemporary of the war. They fix the date by calculation to 1181 B.C. The founder of Buddhism lived in the sixth century B.C. and it can be learnt from the Annals of Magadha that 35 kings reigned between the *Kuru-Panchala* war and the time of Buddha. This would place the war in the thirteenth century B.C. at the latest.

In his work "Early Hindu Civilization", Mr. R.C. Dutt has written that *Sita* and *Rama* of the Ramayana are mythical names, the one the emblem of field-furrow and the other only a new edition of *Indra* battling with the demons of drought. He places the Ramayana as long posterior to the Mahabharata, because he has missed in the Ramayana the fiery valour and the proud self-assertion of the *Kshatriyas* of the Mahabharata. This view of the evolution of ancient society in India can hardly be accepted. Society advances from a simple and rustic to a complicated and enlightened state. The heroes of the Ramayana, still worshipped mostly throughout the northern and southern parts of India cannot be disposed of as mere mythical names. They display the high qualities and ideas of that age, the *yoga,* and are personages of a somewhat tame and simple disposition. The Mahabharata depicts a fine idea of *Jus in personem* and *Jus in rem* among its heroes and a deep logical argument for the war and an elaborate array of arms on both sides which preceded the war. Tradition has it, that the enactments in the Ramayana belong to the *Tretayuga* and those in the Mahabharata to *Dwapar* which followed it. Taking this view, the enactments of the Ramayana were anterior to and no less real than those described in the Mahabharata. The development of society and the establishment of a wider suzerainty in Bharatvarsha at the time of the Mahabharata, were more clearly established than at the time of the Ramayana. The time of the Ramayana must therefore go further backward than that of the Mahabharata.

The succession of kings of the Surjavansa, is given in Bk. 9, chapter XII. of Bhagbat.* The line of succession given below fixes the time of Harischandra 32 generations above Ramchandra, the hero of the Ramayana.

1. Brahma
2. Marichi
3. Kasyapa
4. Surya
5. Sradhadeb (Mann)
6. Ikshaku
7. Nikumbha
8. Indrabahu (Kakuthstha)
9. Anena
10. Prithu
11. Biswarandhi

*Supplied by Pundit Harihar Badopadhya.

12. Chandra
13. Jubanaswa
14. Srabasta
15. Brihadaswa
16. Kubalayaswa
17. Dridaswa
18. Haryaswa
19. Nikumbha
20. Barnaswa
21. Krishaswa
22. Senajit
23. Jubanaswa
24. Mandhata
25. Purukutsa
26. Trasadasya
27. Anaranya
28. Aruna
29. Nibanchana
30. Satyabrata
31. Harischandra
32. Rohitaswa
33. Harita
34. Champa
35. Sudeba
36. Bijoy
37. Bharuka
38. Brika
39. Bahuka
40. Sagara
41. Asamanjas
42. Angshuman
43. Dilipa
44. Bhagiratha
45. Sruta
46. Nava
47. Sindhudipa
48. Ajutaya
49. Rituparna
50. Sarbakam
51. Sudasa
52. Asmaka
53. Narikabacha
54. Dasaratha
55. Oirabida
56. Biswasaha
57. Khattanga
58. Dirghabahu
59. Raghu
60. Prithuraba
61. Aja
62. Ramchandra
63. Kusha

64. Atithi
65. Nishadha
66. Nabha
67. Pundarika
68. Khemadhanwa
69. Debanika
70. Ashiba
71. Pariatra
72. Bajranava
73. Swagan
74. Bidhriti
75. Hirnnyanabha
76. Pushya
77. Dhrubasandhi
78. Sighra
79. Maru
80. Prasusruta
81. Sandhi
82. Amarshana
83. Mahaswana
84. Prasenajit
85. Takhaka
86. Brihatbala
87. Brihadrana
88. Urukriya
89. Batsabridha
90. Pratibyoma
91. Bhanu
92. Dibaka
93. Bahinipati
94. Sahadeba
95. Bira
96. Brihadaswa
97. Bhanuman
98. Pratikasya
99. Sumatrika
100. Marudeba
101. Sunakshatra
102. Pushkara
103. Antariksha
104. Sutapa
105. Amitrajit
106. Brihadasha
107. Barhi
108. Kritanjaya
109. Rananjaya
110. Sanjaya
111. Sudbotha
112. Khudraka
113. Ranaka
114. Suratha
115. Sumitra

The time when Raja Harischandra and his son Rohitaswa lived may be conjectured from the line of kings mentioned above. The period of Rohitaswa goes back thirty-one generations from that of Ramchandra and connects Rohtasgarh with that ancient history of Bharatvarsha.

Topographical

The ancient country known as *Mayadh, Matsya* and *Karus desha* spreads on both sides of the river Sone from its confluence with the Ganges higher up about the Chitrakut Hills, the eastern end of the Vindya Range. On this tract *i.e.* in the south of the present district of Shahabad, stands the Rohtas Hill. The Sone rises together with the Narmuda and the Mahanadi in the elevated plateau of Central India near Amarkantak and runs 325 miles through a high rocky tract receiving tributaries only from the south. On the north the drainage area of the river is limited by the steep slopes and precipices of the Kaimur Range, along which the river flows. After quitting the elevated rocky region of Central India, the Sone river enters the valley of the Ganges and by a straight course of 100 miles, through the plains of South Bihar, joins the sacred river between

Arrah and Patna. The chief peculiarity in the latter portion of its course is its great width which is more than two miles for the greater part of the last 100 miles; while opposite Tilothu it actually attains a breadth of 3 miles. The river Sone nowhere enters the Shahabad district but bounds it on the South and East separating it from the districts of Palamou, Gaya and Patna. It first touches Shahabad near Koshdira a place about 440 feet above the sea and after gradually curving round the Kaimur hills on the west, passes Akbarpur 40 feet lower. Opposite Hankorpur it is joined by the river Koil from Palamou. A species of small pebbles or agates is found below the junction of the Koil. Many of these are ornamental and take a good polish but the majority consist of opaque and diaphanous, silicious rocks. The crystals are very imperfect and generally adhere together in a confused mass. Some are of a reddish tinge, others of a dark green.

The Fort of Rohtas, so-called from the young Prince Rohitaswa, son of Harischandra, stands upon the rock 3 leagues in circumference, facing Koil from its southern end. It is lofty and craggy and contains lakes, woods, pastures, meadows, arable and woodland.

The shape and size of the Rohtas Hill will be seen from the 1 inch to the mile scale map (Plate I). The height of the Hill is 1483 feet from the top of which the river Sone encircling the District of Shahabad to the south and east, appears close to its foot with the intervening ground of verdure and waste as if it is a sheet of velvet in diversified colour. A small hill stream, Aosani Nudi, encircles the foot of the Hill towards the north. Thus the tableland of Rohtas is separated from the plain by natural watery barriers on all sides except the western point, where Kariari Kho and Gularia Kho meet the neck of the Hill cut through to make an artificial barrier as described below. From the midst the tableland extends Soal Sote, a streamlet running north to south and discharging its water in a 'gorge', on the southern verge of the Hill. The northern part of the plateau is covered by pine forests towards the east, and red soil and paddy fields towards the west. The road that stretches over the tableland from east to west crosses Soal Sote and extends through the neck by which Rohtas is connected with the Kaimur mountain ranges.

The two of the principal *Ghats* of the tableland are towards the east and south, known as *Mirara*

Ghat and *Raj-Ghat* leading to the river Sone. (Plate II). The third to the north is called *Ghora-ghat*. The Fort gate at *Mirara Ghat* is reached from Akbarpur, a village below at the foot of the Hill. The ascent from Akbarpur, commonly used, is over dry hills, covered with scrubby brushwood, cut in places to make the ascent comparatively easier. At the top there are some rough steps from ledge to ledge, and gap to gap, well-guarded with walls and an archway of solid masonry. This is all the construction at *Mirara Ghat* gate. Standing on the gate at *Mirara Ghat* we find the sides of the Hill exceedingly steep and there are points which have been rendered inaccessible by stone walls.

It is not easy to go round the whole boundary, which is about 26 miles, to find in how many places such constructions were made and in what condition they remain at present.

Entering upon the tableland from *Mirara Ghat*, the part occupied by the fortress looks well defended both by natural and artificial works. A deep and wide reces, called Kariari Kho, separates this part of the tableland (about 4 miles from east to west and 5 miles from north to south), from that on the north and a branch of this recess, named Gularia Kho, separates it from the tableland to the west leaving only between its south end and the rock that overhangs the, river Sone, a rocky neck about two hundred yards wide. Two sides of this neck are perpendicular, and the sides of the whole circumference are not only everywhere exceedingly steep, but in most places have on some part of their height a perpendicular rock 50 to 150 feet high. The vulnerable part of the fortress is indeed the neck, by which it is joined to the tableland, called Kathotiya (Plate III). So far as can be judged from what remains, it would appear that the Hindus at other places had trusted entirely, or in great measure, to the natural strength of the place but across the neck a wide ditch had been dug into the solid rock and this is said to have been done by the Hindus. According to tradition it was the intention to have made this ditch, very deep, even to the level of the plain, but when a little had been dug, blood issued from a stone and the work was abandoned. The work has indeed every appearance of unfinished rudeness and the stone whence the blood came out was an object of worship so long as the Hindus held the place.

The neighbouring peasants still occasionally bestow on it a little vermilion (red lead) and consider it as the power protecting Rohtas. Two fine gates, one about 30 yards within the other, defend the north side of the neck, which is below the level of the plateau and attached to each by many winding passages, bulwarks, and half-moons, while both of these and the ditch are commanded by a double line of bulwarks, half-moons and curtains with fine battlements, which rise along a low hill, that occupies the south side of the neck and tower 60 or 70 feet above the ditch and recesses for about 400 yards in extent. The access to the different works and communications between them are exceedingly difficult. Although it is said that there were in the fortress a great many guns it does not appear that these works are fitted for receiving them. The embrasures seem to have been fitted for arrows or musketry, although there are a few holes perhaps a foot square, through which small cannon may have been thrust. This part is known as Sing *Darwaj* (Plate III). These works completely command a rising ground within 200 yards to the west. At the east end of the same neck is another line of works called Lal Darwaja *i.e.* red gate, from the colour of some of the stones with which it was built.

Other fortifications are inferior to those at Kathotiya. *Raj Ghat* towards the south, which was the easiest ascent, faces a very steep and high hill, and even there it has been necessary or a considerable way to ascend a perpendicular rock by means of a stair. The works even there are numerous and strong and scarcely visible from below and, in all probability could have been little affected by cannon. Opposite Raj Ghat is *Gazi Darwaja* not far from Habbas Khan's Mosque and Tomb. It may be of later construction. It closes the way to *Ghora Ghat* (Plate IV).

No less than 83 passages, besides the neck, are accessible to men. Three of these and the neck are called the four great *Ghats*, described above, while 80 of more difficult access are called *Ghatis*. Although everyone of these has been more or less fortified and some of them very strongly, yet it is evident that such a place must have always been liable to surprise.

About a mile from the *Mirara Ghat* gate, lies the site of the Temple on the south-east corner of the plateau. There is no trace of the original ancient temple but the site is there. At a short distance from the first step of the stairs to the existing temple, there is a *Stupa,* which is believed by some people as the site of the ancient temple. That this ancient structure was worshipped by men is not much doubted. Nothing more can be said of the little *Stupa.* Dr. Buchanon Hamilton, during his research, found a large and shapeless heap of stones about 20 ft high at the foot of the stairs, which was supposed to be the oldest ruins in the whole place.

The present Temple, which attracts the traveller's eyes, is the foremost object to be seen on the hill and represents the ancient monument of Rohitaswa (Plate V).

It is situated on a steep peak 1400 feet from the foot of the hill, commanding a magnificent view of the country beyond the river Sone. The 84 steps by which one can reach the temple are divided into 12 flights of 7 steps each, with a broad step connecting them. Underneath the stairs there are 11 arched openings. The stairs terminate with a rectangular flat surface from the end of which the plain below is a steep precipice. A few clean steps again conduct to a higher octagonal yard just in front of the temple. This was the audience hall, underneath this surface there are two rooms still existing. The large audience hall, which stood in front of the temple, bore a dome on pillars of stone, which is no longer in existence. The stones lying about there show the nature of the structure that time has pulled down.

The Temple stands in front of the hall. Its crest, it appears, has fallen down. The roof, 2b' feet from the floor, slants towards the four walls and contains a hole at the centre of the ceiling. On the floor there is a nicely cut square cistern of stone in the midst of which the *Lingum* stood. On the northern outer wall of the Temple, there is a sculpture known as the image of Rohitaswa, upon which the water from the cistern inside the temple, pours down through a hole.

It does not appear from all that remain, as has been explained by the antiquarians, that Rohitaswa was the figure which was worshipped by men in this temple. All water that was poured upon the *Lingum* to worship passed through the hole upon the head of the image of Rohitaswa whose resuscitation by the Grace of God (Dharmaraj) was memoralized here and represented by the temple built to commemorate him for ages to come. The stairs were built by Man Sing but the Temple looks much older. Dr. Buchanon Hamilton, judging from the various sculptures, refers it to the three Rajas, who dug the tanks probably in the eleventh century.

Towards the eastern end of the rectangular basement upon which the Temple and audience hall stood, a Mosque with three domes was erected by Emperor Aurangzeb to whom the removal of the idol from the Temple is imputed.

Since the time when the Archaeological Department commenced the restoration of ancient monuments, the Mosque behind the Temple was allowed to stand. But the restoration to its truest character commenced during the Viceroyalty of Lord Curzon of Keddlestone. The interest which Lord Curzon, then the Viceroy and Governor General of India, evinced to preserve the relics of antiquity in India, is known to all. It was that great Viceroy who during his visit to this temple in the year 1903 (January) noticed the desecration of the Hindu temple by the construction of the Mosque adjoining to it and ordered its demolition. Then the Mosque was blown out, and the Temple now stands in its sacred bareness. These works of Lord Curzon will alone keep green his memory in India for ages yet to come.

At the foot of the stairs there is a small temple standing almost in tact. It is a graceful building consisting of a small pillared hall covered with five domes. The image, formerly worshipped here, was also removed by Aurangzeb.

The fortification which has been described above and containing the buildings and temples within, was taken up by Emperor Sher Shah Suri. He captured the Fort in 1539, but the work had but only slightly progressed when he selected a more favourable site for a Fort in the neighbourhood. The fortification walls indicate that the structure was of the time of Sher Shah Suri. The description of the structure of that period is contained in the following passage in Alexander, Cunningham's "Archaeological Survey of India."

"The buildings of Sicandar Lodi and Sher Shah Suri are at once distinguished from those of the Tughluk by their perpendicular walls. Colour was extensively employed for both inside and outside decorations, especially in the grounds or hollows of the stucco medallions and arabesque traceries. Glazed tiles were also used but sparingly at first, for borders and small panels..........During the reign of the Suri family the stucco ornamentation was given up and a much richer and more lasting effect was obtained by the use of different coloured stones, red, white, grey and black. To this period belong the great Masjid in the Fort of Indopat called Killa-kona, Jumma-Masjid near the Qutab Minar and the Moth-ki-Masjid in old Delhi. For other buildings of this style, we have the well-known tombs of Sher Shah Suri and his father Hossen Khan at Saseram and the two gateways called *Delhi Darwaja* and *Lal Darwaja* of Sher Shah's new city of Delhi."

The buildings and other structures indicate works, some executed before the time of Sher Shah Suri and some after he selected his new site for a Fort. The former belonged to the Hindu Rajas and the latter to Man Sing who made his palace here while deputed as Governor of Bengal.

Passing from the Temple to the Palace there is another gate called *Bangla Daroja* (Plate VI). Inside the gate lie three old tanks. The old tanks, named after Ben Raja, Gour Raja and Chandrabhan, are works of the Hindu Rajas who are supposed to have built the temple. It has been thought that these persons were Brahmans, from the last of whom Sher Shah Suri took the place, but this hypothesis is rendered doubtful by the inscription at *Bandhu Ghat Gate*. On the bank of the three tanks stands a majestic mango tree with a trunk 12 feet in height and 18 feet in circumference, which throws its shade far and wide.

The Palace which is the principal building about the place has been fully described in Robert Montgomery Martin's "History of Antiquity, Topography and Statistics of Eastern India", published in 1838.

The Palace or *Mahal Sarai* extends from north to south and has its principal front to the west. It is irregularly built without any architectural pretensions. The whole structure is divided into a number of compartments. Perhaps the most elegant part in the whole is the door—A large Gothic arch with the figure of an elephant on each side. Inside is another arch of equal dimensions, leading into the guard room, one of the best proportioned parts of the whole building. Its roof is plastered in the alcove form, with many small compartments similar to the stone roof in an English Cathedral.

The other compartments of this large building are said to be wanting in symmetry but, as they are, grotesquely magnificent. The whole place has no appearance of monotony and the ingress and egress to all the compartments have been made successfully intricate. The heights of the buildings and the domes supported by stone pillars in some of the courts look majestic.

Each of the compartments has its specific importance more for its purpose than for its making. They can be better appreciated by seeing them. They are as follow: (1) Guard room, the entrance gate. (2) *Baradwari,* the office. (3) Parades for the guards. (4) *Rashun Suhedba Chawk* containing the tomb of a martyr. (5) The abode of the eunuchs. (6) The place where women waited in the open galleries for admission into eunuchs lodgings. (7) *Cis Mahal,* the principal seat of the chief's grandeur and pleasures; *Phul Mahal,* the ladies apartment. (8) A Reservoir with a jet of water. (9) Kitchens. (10) A general route of communication. (11) Apartments for male domestics of the Raja. (12) Reservoir of water. (13) Baths hot and cold. (14) Accommodation to dress and refresh the dancers. (15) Emperor's throne. (16) *Khanabag,* flower garden. (17) *Aynah Mahal,* mirror of palaces. (18) *Naubat.* And (19) An aqueduct to bring water into the garden.

Towards the north of the building there was an egress but now closed up. Towards the east, outside, there is a well with water not far deep. The privies are towards the northern end of the eastern portion of the palace.

The walls are constructed of squared stone, built in an irregular manner. The roofs consist of stone beams and flags covered with plaster. The walls in most parts have been plastered and painted with glaring colours. Man Sing, aware of the people among whom he was placed, introduced nothing of the Hindu mythology into the ornaments except the two elephants on the gate of the Palace and a griffin on the gate at Khathotya, which might in the least affect the most scrupulous Moslem.

There are two inscriptions on the Palace gate and at Khathotya of which a translation in English is given below.

History of the gate of the Mosoliam situated at the foot of the hills

In the reign of His August Majesty Emperor Shah Jahan the Governorship of the fortress with the ranks *Seh Hazari* and *Fojdari* (extending) from Mekrain, P. Siris and Qutambo up to Benares and the *Jagir* of Perganabs *Joudoo, Mankorore, Talaithoo, Akbarpore, Belownja, Bijaigarh* and *Chahla* was conferred on His Highness Nawab Akhlas Ḵhan; and on the humblest of the Slaves of God who was his Son, the Superintendentship of the fortress of Rohtas, and the Fojdari of the villages, and environs of the Fort was bestowed. About this time he died, it therefore so occurred to him (his Son) that during his life time, he laid the foundation of a Platform, a Mosque, boundary walls, underground house, and garden towards the north and south. The construction of the buildings began on the 5th of Rabi-ul-Akhir 1046 A.H. and was completed on the 27th of Ramzan 1047 A.H. Within the boundary walls there is a Mosque, on the walls of which *Ayet Atal-kursi* is engraved, "He is the God, and there is no God except Him, and He is the living and eternal, neither slumber nor sleep seizeth Him. To Him belongeth whatsoever is in Heaven &c. &c."

On the gate of the Rohtas house which has the pomp and grandeur of a Royal Mansion to look at, the statues of elephants are placed. On that building which has its gate towards the south and appears like a Royal Mansion, the following date is engraved:

"This engraving in the reign of His August Majesty Sultan Mohamed Akbar Shah, may God perpetuate his sovereignty and kingdom. When the construction of this strong gate was completed, the gate of Heaven could not vie with it. When I wrote the year of its construction it came to my mind, that Raja Man Singh was its founder On the margin—*Promat Sridhar Daroga Bal Bahadur*—a Brahmin architect and a great master. Written on the 27th of Rajab 1005 A.H. The date of the Mosque of Habbash Khan which is superbly magnificent and is situated towards the east of the grand *Rauza*. The brave Akbar, that through his dignity, his horse traverses the high firmament. In the reign of such an Emperor that beasts and birds are under his command, it was in the mind of Habbash Khan that he should construct a Mosque for the general good. The year of the date of this existing Mosque came out by reckoning, "the abode of good" (Baqai Khair), on the 6th of Rajab 986 A.H."

From the west gate of the palace compound, *Rajghat* is about a mile. There are two temples which fall on the way. Gonesh Temple is one of them exceedingly handsome, being covered by a dome, which surpasses in lightness all the Hindu works that Dr. Buchanon Hamilton had ever seer. The other is smaller and dedicated to some *Tirthankara* of the Jains. It is at *Rajghat* the stairs were constructed to descend on the plain. The architecture there is worthy of notice.

Within the gate at *Rajghat* there must have been a very considerable building, which is thought to have formed the private residence of the commander. In it are two temples both attributed to Man Singh.

Three-fourths of a mile from the north gate of the palace compound lie Habbash Khan's Mosque and Tomb. The tomb lies in a building 48' 6" square with an elevation of 65 feet. On the four corners of the compound, 96 feet square, there are four small hexagonal guard rooms one of which leads to a circular reservoir 54 feet in diameter and 6 feet deep. This was maintained to water the place and the garden. The Mosque lies to the west of the tomb. Beyond these two structures towards the north, lies the way which leads to Gazi Darwaja described above.

On the road to Kathotya, at a distance of about 2½ miles from the west gate of the Palace, Juma Masjid is situated to the left. Juma Masjid is an edifice of 40 feet in height with 3 domes, the diameter of the central one is 24 feet and of those on the two sides of it, 21 feet each. This building has undergone repairs. This is attributed to the time of Sher Shah Suri as the Rauza of Habbash Khan described above. Structures with hemispherical domes supported on pillars and octagonal halls covered by hemispherical domes, which are found in front of some Hindu temples here, are importations from the west. They were evidently introduced by the garrison of the Fort who came there with Sher Shah Suri or Raja Man Singh.

At a short distance from the western Palace gate, another temple is situated a little way off to the right from the road to Kathotya. The temple stands adjoining to an apartment with a hemispherical dome which is approached by a few steps. Inside the temple a smell of gunpowder was perceived, from which it is now called the gunpowder temple.

At a little distance from the Palace, between the roads to *Rajghat* and Kathotya, a path stretches to Shah Babul Syed's tomb. This Mahomedan saint was interred in a cave overlooking a perpendicular precipice about 1000 feet high. The cave lies on the western side of the plateau where the water from *Bhuki Kho* discharges in a gorge. A few winding steps down the side of the plateau lead to a low corridor, a few yards in length and just enough for a man to crawl into the cave. The space inside the cave can accommodate hundreds of men. The awe inspiring sight in front of the corridor is due to the situation of the cave at the head of a ravine. Opposite to the cave there is a well, cut much below on the side of the hill.

There is no other place on the hill to which the attention of the traveller may be drawn. There were villages and corn fields on the plateau of which clear evidence is still available. Water was said to have been found in abundance. The well behind the Palace contains water within a few feet from its top.

There are also some small channels (called Kho) which discharge the rainwater to the plains below. *Babhan Talao nadi* falls into *Koala Kho* which separates a small peak at the north-eastern corner of the plateau on which is situated the temple of Rohitaswa. Close by, to the east of the Palace are *Tost Kho* which carries off the excess water from the 3 historical tanks commonly called *Gotalao, Babhan Talao* and *Kamal Daha,* and *Mangoo Kho,* which commences from *Lalooa Pahari*.

Fine trees and paddy lands lie between *Aosani Nadi* and the road to Kathotya. Mango, mohua, plum, aora, tern and peal are the fruit trees on the Hill. Cultivable lands are settled with the residents @ Els. 2 to Us. 6 per *Bigha.* The right to levy *Banskati* dues is also settled. The inhabitants of the place are Dhangar, Ahir and Bhuia. All *Jait* raiyats have Jagir lands. Heavy rains last for 4 months. In summer the days are not very trying.

Rohtas Pargana is over 500 square miles in extent and includes the greater part of the Kaimur plateau in the Sassaram Sub-division. Rohtas plateau is a *Khas Mahal* with rights of a *Banskati Mahal*. From Kathotya the road stretches to Sergarh through Rehal, a distance of 20 miles. Sergarh was selected by Sher Shah Suri as a better site than Rohtas for building a Fort.

The author of the Seir Mutaqherin considers Chunargar, although a fortress upon a rock, is not to be compared with Goaliar, Rohtas, Gandicota and others, for he says it has no ground within itself capable of providing the subsistance of a garrison, nor has it so many other conveniences. How the fortress of Rohtas is now a *Khas Mahal* will be dealt within the historical portion.

Historical

The Rohtasgarh has its history connected with the Hindu, Mahomedan and British rule of the country.

Little or nothing is known concerning the persons who held the Fort from the time of Harischandra up to 1100 A.D. Harischandra lived 32 generations behind Ramchandra. The date of the Mahabharata and that of the compilation of the Vedas have been discussed sufficiently accurately and fixed by historians. No historian has fixed the date of the story of Ramayana. That the war waged by Ramchandra against Ravana, the King of *Lankadwip* (Ceylon) is older than the wars of Kuru-Pandab described in the Mahabharata admits of not much doubt. The following quotation from Mountstuart Elphinstone's history of India throws some light on the antiquity of Ramayana. "The author, Valmiki is said to have been contemporary with the event; but not even a poet would invest a living warrior with supernatural powers, and would give him an army of apes for allies. A considerable time must have elapsed before the real circumstances of the story were sufficiently forgotten to admit of such bold embellishments. This argument however shows the early date of the hero, without impugning the antiquity of the poem."

In the great epic of Ramayana, the song of love of truth and duty was sung yet unknown anywhere in the world. This heavenly age gradually levelled down into what we read of the strife described in the Mahabharata about 1400 B.C. Small principalities sprung up all over Hindusthan displaying envy and malice, disregard of honesty and truth which Lord Krishna, the great *Abatar* and a principal Hero of the Mahabharata subdued not without great loss of mankind. He waged his wars in the *Magadh, Matsya* and *Karus desk* and, as tradition has it, encamped in Harigram now known as Hargaon near the present-day Karisath station. Who knows that Rohtas Fort was not connected with the warfare down to that period about the thirteenth to fourteenth century B.C. Gautam Buddha was born in the sixth century before Christ. The seat of his work was not far remote from Rohtas. But we read no mention of this ancient place in the Chinese travellers Fa Hian's or Houen Tsang's account of India who visited the country in the fourth and seventh century after Christ.

Nor Megasthenes who cams to India and resided in the Royal Court of Chandragupta in Pataliputra between 317 and 312 B.C. made mention of Rohtas. So far is clear that a thousand years before Ramchandra, Raja Harischandra of the Solar dynasty was the great hero of one of the most beautiful legend of Hindu mythology. The exploits of Ramchandra, and Sri Krishna narrated in the epics of Ramayana and Mahabharata are matters of history down to the 13th and 14th century B.C. They were followed by Gautama Buddha. What changes the character of men underwent during these early centuries have been folly discussed by historians. Since that remote age when Harischandra lived down to 1100 A.D., Rohtas has not been mentioned in any work now extant.

In Robert Montgomary Martin's, "History of Antiquity, Topography, and Statistics of Eastern India", we have the following passages.

"Whether or not Rohitaswa resided there may be doubtful but his image, there can be little doubt, continued to be worshipped in the fortress until destroyed by the zeal of Aurangzeb; such at least is the general tradition and all the circumstances are highly probable." "Very little indeed remains that can be attributed to the Hindus. Near the palace are 3 old tanks called after Ben Raja, Gour Raja and Chandrabhan. Many think that these were 3 persons of the same family by caste Brahmans and that it was from Chandrabhan that Sher Shah Suri took the place..........345 years intervening between the death of Jaya Chandra and the capture of

Rohtasgarh by Sher Shah Suri will not only admit of the 12 Governors mentioned in the inscriptions, but of the 3 Brahmans. The silence, however, of the inscription concerning these persons, while it goes on to mention the tributaries who held the country after the conquest, is a strong circumstance against the truth of this tradition; and if any such persons as Ben, Gour and Chandrabhan existed, which from the circumstance of the tanks is not improbable, they may have held Rohtas after Pratap Dhanala, and in fact the Belonja Raja who pretends to be this person's descendant, alleges that he was the great-grandson of Chandrabhan."

A rock-cut inscription at Phulwari dated 1164 A.D. refers to the construction of a road up to the Hill by Pratap Dhanala, the chief of Japla, evidently mordern Japla, 8 miles from Rohtasgarh on the opposite bank of the Sone river. Another inscription near *Lal Darwaja* dated 1223 A.D. mentions a descendant of Pratap Dhanala.

In Tariki-Sher-Shah Suri the following account is given regarding Rohtas and its occupation by Sher Shah Suri.

According to Ferishta's account it is manifest that there was none in the family of the Raja of Rohtas to survive him and so his dynasty was altogether extinct: the high officials and nobles of the Delhi throne did not permanently settle towards this side they being attaches to the Governor of Behar whose headquarter was at Azimabad. But some camp followers of Humayun's force, who had accompanied him, as mercenary soldiers from Persia, where he had taken shelter after his defeat by Sher Shah Suri, appear to have settled in this Parganah known as Traki, a Province of Persia. This is easily traceable from their national epithet which they still retain.

"Sher Khan left Ghazi Sur and Bulaki, who was the commandant of Chunar, in that fortress and removed his family and those of his Afgan followers to the fortress of Bahrkudas; but as he had many families with him that Fort could not hold them all. There existed a friendly connection between Sher Khan and the Raja of the Fort of Rohtas. Churamon, the Raja's *Naib* was on terms of intimate friendship and alliance with Sher Khan. This Churamon was a Brahman and was a person of the highest rank and had formerly shown kindness to the family of Mia Nizam, brother of Sher Khan and procured his shelter in the Fort of Rohtas and when all danger had gone by, the family again quitted the Fort and it was made over to the Raja. But on this occasion the

Raja declined to admit Sher Khan's family into his Fort. Churamon went to the Raja and said "It is not becoming of your dignity to break your promise; Sher Khan on the strength of it, has brought his families from the Fort of Bahrkuda." When the Raja saw Churamon thus determined, he agreed to admit the family of Sher Khan into the Fort. Sher Khan brought his women and children near to the Fort and expressed his devoted friendship for and obligation to the Raja and gave him much money and goods of various kinds. The Raja was much delighted and said, "The Fort of Rohtas is yours, order in your family." Sher Khan thanked God and said; "I was not so pleased at the conquest of Gour, as I am at getting possession of Rohtas." Sher Khan placed his own guards and sentries at every part of the Fort and took the greatest precaution for its safe custody and drove the Raja away from the Fort."

The commonly received report that Sher Khan put Afghans into *dolis,* (litters) and sent them into the Fort as women is all together erroneous and false.

The *doli* story runs thus:—There were 1200 litters, in each of which were two Afghans armed, except in some of the foremost in which there were old women. After the examination of some of the leading litters, Sher Khan sent a message to the Raja, to represent that the Raja having now satisfied himself that there were only women in the litters and as it was highly scandalous to expose them to the gaze of the sentries, the search ought to be discontinued. The Raja readily assented and when the litters had all been introduced and discharged their burdens, the Afghans took possession of the gates and admitted Sher Shah Suri who was ready with his army outside, awaiting the successful result of his stratagem.

Emperor Sher Shah Suri is said to have constructed a new Rohtas. This is described in page 114 of the History of India, as told by its historians—the posthumous papers of the late Sir H.M. Elliot K.C.B. edited and continued by professor John Dawson M.R.A.S. Staff College Sandhurst. The new Rohtas as described in this History, it seems, referred to Shergarh, twenty miles west of Rohtas, which might have been the place to oppose the passage of the Mughals.

"Constructs new Rohtas—Its cost—Khizir Khan, Governor of Bengal.

Sher Shah Suri threatened to construct such a Fort in that country that it should not only effectually restrain the Ghokkars, but also the passage of the Mughals. He therefore himself made a tour through the hills *Girjhak Ninduna* (mountains circumdacent), and finding a fit spot, he laid the foundations of the Fort, which he called Rohtas."

"Sher Shah Suri issued *farmans* to complete the fortifications of Rohtas; but Todar Khatri represented that the Ghokkars, to whom that country belonged, would not allow any one to work for wages; and that they had agreed amongst themselves, upon oath, to expatriate every person that should contravene their wishes. Sher Shah Suri, in answer, told him (that he should in noways be allowed to give up that work, which he only wished to do in consequence of his greediness for gold), that the work did not seem to advance under his superintendence, an that a man who was fond of money, and was alarmed about disbursing it, would never accomplish the king's designs, Todar, on the reception of this fresh command, fixed first a golden *ashrafi* as the enormous remuneration for one stone, which induced the (kakers) Ghokkars to flock to him in such numbers that afterwards a stone was paid with a *rupee,* and this pay gradually fell to five *takas,* till the fortress was completed."

If this new Rohtas was the Sher Garh, it is described below. Sher Shah Suri found its situation better than that of Rohtas-Garh, which all about the place go to prove. It was, however as it seems, meant more for a shelter after defeat than a place from where he could keep the enemy at bay; for it could not accommodate a garrison or stand a protracted siege.

Sher Garh Fortress

An undulating ground across two hill streams extending over a distance of about five miles, intervenes between Malhipur and the foot of the hill on which was built the fortress of Sher Garh. The passage across the hill stream, Dandanoa, has been cut out deep enough to bewilder a traveller. The bed of the stream is flat like plains not more than 50 feet in width through which the rush of water during the rainy months is in itself an awful spectacle. Between this river and the foot of the hills there are low chasms, diversified with cultivated spots, which no doubt present a pleasant sight to one who can cross the Dandanoa in the rains. At the foot of the hill leaving the Durgaoti river on one side and *Badargar Kho* on the other, through a most mysterious toe-path, in which people are often misled, nature presents a nice platform to the traveller as if for his rest. From there he can fairly find his own situation and begin to ascend the hill. From the landing the first gate to the Fort is reached by series of steps in number 12, 18, 25, 27, 29, 60, 50, and 26 in each series. Each step is from 20 feet to 30 feet wide and a foot high. Inside the gateway there is a large apartment for soldiers with 6 nice stalls for sentinels on the roof. From this gate to the second it is a long walk of descent and ascent on the plateau. The ascent terminates at a point just below the second gate where there lies a tank 200 feet square with high masonry walls on all sides, except the west, opening out in a gorge down to the Durgaoti river. From the tank the entrance of the second gate is reached by a flight of 38 steps of which 4 have crumbled down. The passage through the gateway is 11 feet wide in front and 18 feet inside; on each side of the passage where it is 18 feet wide, two long open porticoes extend.

From this point the third gate of the Fort is reached by 80 short, steep but clear steps. This is a steep ascent at the top of which lies a flat roof of concrete. Underneath this roof there are a well and a dark cell. By 10 steps downwards the well is reached. The well is covered by a masonry hemispherical dome supported on pillars. There is a promenade 9 feet wide all round with 12 openings towards the well covered with an arched roof. One opening by which the cell underneath the roof of concrete can be reached admits so little light that nothing can be seen there except with the help of a torch. What it was intended for cannot be known. It was a place to conceal is clear enough. From this point up to the foot of the steps leading to the last gate of the Fort is a gentle ascent protected on both sides by walls. To the left of this passage there is a Mosque almost dilapidated hanging on the bed of the Durgaoti river and to the right a door opens out to a staircase down to the tank described above. This staircase is not intact and cannot be used for the purpose for which it was intended. At the end of this gentle slope, there are 20 steps to ascend upon the front court of underground buildings, 300 feet square. Behind this court, there is another court a little below the level of the former, 130 feet square. The former was evidently the male apartment and the latter the female apartment. This whole area is surrounded on all sides by a steep precipice down to the bed of the Durgaoti river. There is a door to the extreme west from which the passage down to the bed of the Durgaoti river appears inaccessible.

The whole area on the hill occupied by the Sher Garh Fort has neither any natural source of supply of water nor any ground to cultivate. It could not accommodate a large garrison. The situation of Sher Garh as a Fort is evidently superior to that of Rohtasgarh, though it is lower in height and much smaller in area than what the latter commands. There is no pasture nor anything like a forest. The rain water is preserved in the well and the tank for use during the whole year. The underground rooms receive light through the opening on the roof from which the steps descend. All these rooms bear signs of more or less decay. The central room was well lighted by means of a skylight but its roof has gone down. Another can be reached by 13 steps downwards containing a square water reservoir surrounded by a wide platform which afforded accommodation for living within; another was almost similar to the second one but is more out of order. There are two other cells much less lighted and might have been used for stores. The construction of the roof was such that it did not admit rainwater into the rooms.

No mention of this fortress is made in connection with any subsequent historical event.

The Fort of Rohtas was under an officer, known as Killadar, who defrayed all expenses from the revenues of the following estates: Chainpur, Sassaram, Kera, Mongasaur Siris, Cootamba, Dugal, Chargauja, Japla, Belonja, Bijoygarh, Akbarpur, Tilothu and Palamou. These states which lie partly in Chota Nagpur and Mirzapur were managed by a special *Dewan.* A guard of 4 or 5 hundred men was granted for the protection of the Fort in addition to which there was the regular military garrison commanded by an officer of 1000 men. This post, which was hereditary, was held originally by Rajputs but since about 1810 the holders were Mahomedans. The garrisons were natives of the fortress whose families, contrary to rules, occupied a small town at the foot of the hill called Akbarpur. Tradition has it that the Rajput soldiers who accompanied Sher Shah Suri had to carry the food prescribed to the Hindus. They could not return to their homes. The Emperor granted them *Jagir* of Akbarpur where they brought their families from home and lived ever since.

When Man Sing was appointed Viceroy of Bengal and Behar by Emperor Akbar, he selected Rohtas as a place of safety for his family and treasures. All the buildings now on the place seem to have been erected by him. Two inscriptions in Sanskrit and Persian on the Palace gate and Kathotya show that these works were finished in the year 1654 A.D. *i.e.* 10 years after Man Sing's appointment as Governor. After his death the fortress was annexed to the office of the Vizier of the empire, "By whom the governors were appointed. It is stated that Habbas Khan lived simultaneously with Man Sing on the hill and he was a favourite commander of the Emperor's army."

Shah Jahan rose in rebellion against his father Emperor Jahangir in 1624. He obtained possession of Bengal and was able to seize on Behar. Pressed by Parviz and Mohobat Khan he was obliged to attend to his own safety which he secured in the Rohtas Garh. His adherents left him and dispirited by ill-health he wrote to beg his father's forgiveness. Emperor Jahangir directed him to give up the Forts of Rohtasgarh and Asirgarh which were in his possession.

The Governor of Rohtasgarh protected Shah Jahan's family until pardon was granted him in 1644 A.D.

Emperor Aurangzeb's attention was drawn to Bengal about 1659, when his son Prince Sultan and Mir Jumla were carrying on operations against Suza. Aurangzeb, who had at one time determined on a journey to Bengal, had given it up before he got the news of his son's alliance with Suza, whose daughter he married. His bigotry was then levelled against the Hindus. It is not known at what time the idols were removed from the temples at Rohtasgarh and a Mosque was built adjoining to the great temple to the east, its sacred side. But it may be supposed that all this was done about the time of Aurangzeb's reign.

Emperor Bahadoor Shah appointed Yzed-dowlah (1707-1713) to the government of Bengal and commanded Ferok Syer's attendance at court. Ferok Syer did not choose to trust himself near the Emperor and prolonged his stay at Azimabad. Just then Mohamed Reja, who fled from Bahadoor Shah's resentment, got by means of a forged order the possession of Rohtas (about 1711 A.D.) and wrote to the Emperor that his soldier, referring to himself, had through the sloth and incapacity of the Governor, found means to get such a post. The Emperor issued orders to Ferok Syer to dispossess the imposter which was done by stratagem. The latter informed Mohamed Reja through Dulachin that order was received from the Emperor to confirm him in his post and so he came with a retinue to the foot of the Hill. He was admitted with only 2 of the retinue and when the *farman* was being read by Mohamed Reja he was stabbed to death. This happened when news had come of Bahadoor Shah's demise.

Jaffar Khan was Dewan of Bengal since Aurangzeb's time. In course of time Azim Ushan, second son of Bahadoor Shah, vested him with the power of Nizam (military government), of the Province. Later on he procured the *Subadarship* of Orissa for his son-in-law Sujah Khan. Jaffar Khan's daughter came away from Sujah Khan with her son Sarfarz Khan in disgust and settled in Murshidabad. Jaffar Khan attempted to appoint his grandson as *Subadar* of Bengal but Sujah Khan with the advice of Aliverdy Khan obtained the patent from the Emperor in his favour and ascended the *musnad,* Sujah Khan's chief councellor was Aliverdy Khan who was deputed by him as Governor of Azimabad.

Sujah Khan, who was then Viceroy of Bengal, Azimabad and Orissa, died about the time when Nadir Shah came to Shahjehanabad (Agra). Sarfarz Khan succeeded him and took possession of the 3 Provinces. Aliverdy Khan did not much trust, and paid little deference to his new master. Aliverdy Khan got the imperial command and proceeded against Sarfarz Khan leaving his youngest nephew and son-in-law for his Deputy and Lieutenant and sending his father to command the district of Siris and Cootomba, where the people were accustomed to respect him. While Aliverdy was employed elsewhere, the Viceroy of Azimabad was undertaking an expedition against the refractory *Zamindars* of Bhojpur in Shahabad and Rohtas. The Raja of Ramgar was the most powerful *Zamindar* of the Hill and was so warlike that the Viceroys of the Province had hardly any control over him. Hedayet Ali with the help of both the *Zamindars* of Palamou and of Siris and Cootomba laid siege to the fortress of Ramgar.

About 1747 A.D. Aliverdy Khan's Deputy conceived the idea of independence and with this view in mind obtained permission of the Viceroy to engage the Afghan soldiers who were expelled from the army. The Governor of Azimabad, who did not listen to the Afghan commander to grant full pardon to the refractory Zamindars with whom he was related, was afterwards murdered by the Afghans. *Zamindars* of Siris and Cootomba then rose up and attacked Medy Nissar Khan, who with the few people that remained with him and the money he had collected, made good his retreat to Rohtas where Ali Khan, the Governor, received him with honour and lodged him in the fortress.

All this happened when Emperor Mahammad Shah died, 1748/49 A.D. Then followed dissension in Aliverdy's family. Seraj-ud-dowla claimed the government of Azimabad as his paternal property and was appointed to that post with Janpkiram as his deputy. He set out for Azimabad with Luft-un-nisa and his mother, where he was well received by Medy Nissar Ali, Governor of Azimabad, Siraj-ud-dowla returned and succeeded Aliverdy Khan on his demise. His enemies were contriving to bring about his fall. Defeated in his engagement with the English he was taken a prisoner.

Mir Jaffar Khan, then Governor of the Province, required Ram Narayan to render a full account of the management of the revenue of Azimabad for many years past. Ram Narayan was in correspondence with Colonel Clive, who prevented Mir Jaffar from his intentions. Ram Narayan on the contrary obtained release of the districts of Belounja and some other lands which Siraj-ud-dowla confiscated and allowed as *jaigir,* hereditary to the family of Naky Ally Khan. It was about this time Sitab Rai was vested with the offices of Imperial Dewan of Azimabad and the government of the fortress of Rohtas, together with the management of Semsam-ud-dowla's *jaigir* lands in Bengal. He arrived at Azimabad shortly after Mir Jaffar had arrived there. He obtained the commander's recommendation in support of the patents he brought from the Imperial Court. Mir Jaffar Khan also recommended him to Ram Narayan. This Governor on seeing him return to Azimabad with such a powerful support installed him in those three offices to which he had been appointed by the Imperial Court.

Naky Ally Khan tired of the endless hopes, which his friend Mir Jaffar Khan continually gave him, returned to Azimabad. The whole province of Azimabad acknowledged no other master than Raja Ram Narayan. As soon as the *Nawab* departed from Azimabad, Ram Narayan resolved to bring under control Raja Bishen Singh, *Zamindar* of Siris and Cootomba, who after Serajuddowla's death refused to pay any rent to the treasury and wanted to become independent. Bishen Singh made some resistance at first but submitted, giving his son Narayan Singh, a boy of twelve years of age, in hostage for the arrears which he owed. Raja Ram Narayan seemed intent on putting in execution Mir Jaffar Khan's order concerning Naky Ally Khan. He spoke much to Bishen Singh on the necessity of his evacuating the Forts and the *jaigir* lands, to Naky Ally Khan. Meanwhile Naky Ally Khan with his small troops marched to Rohtas and forcibly seized the Forts and villages. Raja Ram Narayan wrote to Raja Sunder Singh to support Naky Ally Khan in his rights.

When Ally Gohar, alias Emperor Shah Allam, conducted an expedition against Azimabad, Ram Narayan sought the assistance of the English. He beseiged Azimabad. Beaten there he commanded Sitab Roy's return. He received homage from Mir Kasim and signed a treaty with the Englishman. Ram Narayan's office of Governor of Azimabad was conferred upon Mir Kasim Khan. Mir Kasim Khan undertook to visit the fortress on Rohtas. He informed accordingly Nessar Ali Khan the Governor, as well as Saho Mal, his deputy. The *Nawab*, after having amused himself with a view of the fortress returned, to Sassaram and put under confinement Saho Mal, the deputy Governor of Rohtas as well as Naky Ally Khan, who was for a long time the Governor there. The *Nawab* then appointed Mir Medy Khan to command in the district of Sassaram, and Chainpur, comprising under his management the several *Zamindaries* of Siris Cootomba *etc.* whence their owner Bishen Singh had fled to Benares. He also sent for Raja Rajballav, deputy Governor of Azimabad and put him under safe confinement, and in his stead Raja Nabet Rai was invested with the *khelat* of Azimabad and sent to take care of that province and city.

Mir Kasim Khan fell out with the Englishman, who commenced hostility by plundering the city of Azimabad (1763 A.D.). This was followed by the Nawab's engagement with the Englishman at several places, and when he received the news that his general Mahomed Taki Khan was killed at Kutwa, he took steps to send his seraglio and treasures to the fortress of Rohtas. He dismissed a vast number of women he kept; but his own consort, Mir Jaffir Khan's daughter, together with his favourite ladies and his treasurers were sent to the fortress under the care of Mir Sulaman Khan and Raja Nabet Rai. Mir Kasim's defeat was completed when the strong post he chose at Udaynala was forced open by the Englishman (August 1763).

When Mir Kasim was totally repulsed after his bloody actions and was retreating to Suza-ud-dowla's country and was waiting to give time to his consort and treasures to join him from Rohtas,

Mirza Nabet Khan who escaped from Udaynala, joined him in his camp. Nabet Khan advised him to retire within the fortress of Rohtas, leaving the army and management of war with him. But Mir Kasim objected to the air and water of Rohtas and also to the other proposals made by Nabet Khan. There were a number of covered coaches and chairs which passed for conveyances containing ladies hut in reality contained bags of white cloth, gold, jems and jewels. Mir Sulamon both on going to and coming from the Rohtas, stole and embezzled a large number of jewels. On his return Mir Kasim dismissed his troops, paid them off and directed his route to the Vizier's camp. There Mir Sulamon became an important man. Mir Kasim's whole property was traced by exercising severities upon his women, eunuchs and other dependants and confiscated, except a few jewels of high value he could remove through a trusted servant. Mir Sulaman turned out to be an informer and expressed to the Vizier that he knew all the wealth and effects of Mir Kasim lodged in the fortress of Rohtas and had a scheme ready by which the fortress with all its dependencies and contents might be brought under his power and annexed to his dominions. Mir Sulamon got letters from the Vizier upon Rahim Khan, Governor of

Sassaram and some other principal persons, besides Yakub Khan and Saho Mal, who commanded in Rohtas; and himself arrived there with the letters.

Just at this very time, Major Monro landed at Azimabad and wished to have the fortress of Rohtas put in the hands of the Englishman. Raja Saho Mal was addressed on the subject by Golam Hossin Khan, who was requested by doctor Fullarton to intercede. He wrote to Raja Saho Mal to consider that the ruin of the Vizier by the Englishman was imminent and therefore he should, under the circumstances, makeover the fortress to the Englishman, but in such a manner as not to deliver the fortress to his master's enemies and still less to a traitor. The Raja desired that some Englishman troops under an officer should come there, and that the conditions on which he was willing to surrender the fortress might be signed by the British commander and returned to him. Mir Sulamon remained in suspense all the while. Major Monro signed the conditions and returned the papers. Captain Goddard approached from Ticary with a force to whom the Raja surrendered the fort, with all its contents. Mir Sulamon returned to the Vizier and reported the Facts to him. Saho Mal who had fallen out with Captain Goddard also represented to Golam Hossin Khan that not one of the stipulated conditions had been observed with him. Colonel Goddard remained in the Fort for 2 months and destroyed all the military stores.

Golam Hossin Khan took Saho Mal to Major Monro at Azimabad. The province of Azimabad was divided into eight *Sarkars* viz. Shahabad, Rohtas, Monghyr, Behar, Champaran, Saran, Tirhut and Hazipur. There were two Parganahs in the Teshil or Sarcar of Rohtas, viz. Siris and Cootomba, under the *Zamindari* of Raja Bishen Sing, but owing to various cliques and intrigues the Raj was sold in 1213 Fasli. Raja Saho Mal held the fortress of Rohtas and ruled over all the villages situated within its political boundaries.

As there was no male issue to the Raja, his Rani succeeded him after his death in the year 1213 Fasli. The Parganahs of *Japla* and *Balanza* were bestowed upon Nawab Syed Golam Hossin Khan Bahadoor, author of "Seir Mutaqherin" and Nawab Fakheer-ud-dowla, maternal grandfather of Nawab Hazi Syed Wallayet Ali Khan of Patna. The last-named Nawab is still in possession of the Pargana *Japla* by right of inheritance. The other Parganah has now been leased out on a certain fixed annual rental, and divided between the heirs of the deceased Nawab in proportion to their respective shares.

Saho Mal was the last Killadar-in-charge of Rohtas. He was made Raja by the Britishers. The family was settled in Tilothu. They came from Amorha near Amritsar with the Emperor who settled them in the village. They have got the Badshahi *farman*. The family descendants were Rai Harbans Shahai, Babu Ram Lochan Singh (adopted), Babu Dev Narain Singh, Babu Indra Dewan Singh (adopted) and Minor Radha Prasad Singh, who is now living. Saho Mal, in consideration of his services rendered to the Company, obtained possession of the parganah except the Rohtas Fort and the small plateau on which it stands, which were retained by the Government.

Since the capture of the Rohtas fortress by Colonel Goddard, the place enjoyed tranquillity broken only during the Mutiny. Kunwar Singh of Jagadishpur was the principal mutineer in Shahabad. He engaged with the Englishman at several places and was at last mortally wounded while crossing the Ganges, as some of his followers aver. He was an old man and died three days after he underwent the amputation of his wrist. He was succeeded by his brother Amar Singh. Amar Singh and his followers infested the neighbourhood of the fortress. The mutineers used the Fort as a rallying point and raised a band of men to occupy it. It is said that Amar Singh, who was once living in the Fort, found the European soldiers rushing up from below and made his escape in the disguise of a cowherd, himself directing the soldiers to the Palace to catch Amar Singh there. Thus the real Amar Singh made good his escape. All the rebels were repulsed, who now entered upon the Kaimur Range. The District quieted down by October and November of 1858. When the rebels became aware that they were opposed by troops against whom they could not hope any success in the field, but whom it was even impossible for them to shake off in flight, the restoration of order in the district became an easy task.

Akbarpur, the village at the foot of the Rohtas Hill was given as a life grant to Mr. Vicars Boyle, a civil engineer connected with the Railway, for his memorable services in defending the European residents in his house, at Arrah, during the Mutiny. It may not be out of place to quote a few passages from Kaye's and Mallison's History of the Indian Mutiny regrading his work. "He had from a very early period regarded it as a quite possible contingency that the station might be attacked by the mutineers. He, therefore, despite the jeers of some and the covered ridicule of others, had fortified the smaller of the two houses in his compound, in a manner which would enable it to defend any sort of assault. This house was a small detached building about fifty feet square, having one story above the basement and surmounted by a flat roof. Supplies of all kinds, meal, wine, beer, water, biscuit and sheep had been gradually stored up by Mr. Boyle during the month."

"Additional means of defence were now provided; ammunition was collected, loopholes were drilled in the walls and sandbags were placed on the roof. At the same time the front portion of the other and larger house in the same compound, about fifty yards distant from the improvised fortress, was entirely demolished so as to prevent it from affording shelter to any possible assailants."

There were fifteen Europeans at the station who took shelter in Mr. Boyle's little house. Every means that energy could do, that skill could devise and that valour could attempt were successfully resorted to by that daring garrison, ably directed by Mr. Herwald Wake, Mr. Vicars Boyle and Mr. Calvin. This Mr. Vicars Boyle died on 6th January 1908.

From the perusal of this history it will appear that the fortress of Rohtas was never a scene of action. The fortress was neither, on any occasion beseiged to secure hold upon enemies lodged there nor contained a garrison to fight out enemies outside. The part it has played in the history is no more than to give shelter to fugitive princes and accommodate some important chiefs and *Zamindars* with residential houses. Its connection with the oldest Hindu Temple, the desecration of it by a bigoted Mahommadan Emperor and lastly its restoration from defilement under the orders of His Excellency the Viceroy and Governor General, Lord Curzon of Keddlestone, are rather the principal subjects in its history to be recorded.

History of religion in India is the history of man's struggle to solve man's fundamental spiritual needs. The more modern idea, viz, let religion be relegated to the past, let science develop into perfection, let there be an endeavour to better the condition of man's present life, let material comfort increase, let intellect be cultivated to endow life with beauty and refinement, and let man cease from vain concern about the future and seek not to compass the impossible, was not the idea in that remote age when Raja Harischandra played his part, a time not fixed with certainty by years. Attempt has been made to fix the time by discussing the date of the Mahabharata,—the landmark of ancient history of India—and then pointing out that the Ramayana described incidents of much earlier date. Attempt has been made to explain the *Yugadharma,* the four stages of the evolution of the Hindu religion, each of which must have been the result of thousands of years of study and investigation. The date of the war, described in the Mahabharata, which happened in the *Dwapar-Yuga,* was fixed about the thirteenth century B.C. by antiquarian researches. The exploits of Ramchandra described in the Ramayana happened in the *Treta-Yuga* preceding *Dwapar*. Raja Harischandra's renunciation of all worldly wealth without a feeling of pleasure and pain and his complete devotion to the lowest form of life, have been ascribed to the *Satya-Yuga.* Each Yuga covered an age, 2000 years at the lowest computation. The Solar kings from Harischandra downward might have embraced a period of about 5000 years. The three Yugas coming down to the age of the Mahabharata make up a period of 6 thousand years. Even supposing that the *Kuru-Panchal* war followed close upon the end of the Solar Dynasty, the time for Raja Harischandra's exploits must go back to 6 thousand years B.C. The realization of Soul and its immortality, the ideal that sacrifice pleases God and advancement of spiritual training *i.e.* the higher state of consciousness, we are capable of realising is the aim of life and not the increase of pleasure working with world of matter and motion outside the self, are the proud heritage of modern India. All that is connected with the exploits of Raja Harischandra, point to this high ideal.

The place in ancient India renowned for the exploits of Raja Harischandra was above the Vindhya range, on the tract between the confluence of the Ganges and the Sone. The legends that Raja Trisanku was hurled down by the Gods when ascending to Heaven and his tears flowed as the river Karamnasha and that his son, Harischandra was favoured by the Gods with resuscitation of Rohitaswa, immortalized by the temple on the Rohtas Hills, distinctly prove the sacredness of the region. Who occupied the hills before the time of Harischandra, who built the temple and at what time are matters for research.

Revenue

The Killadar-in-charge of the Fort was vested with certain Parganahs by virtue of his appointment as noted above. The estate was gradually split up. Azimabad was the capital of the territory which comprised Rohtas. *Siris* and Cootomba in the District of Gaya, constituted a portion of the grant were sold in 1213 Fasli. *Japla* and *Belonza* in Palamou District were conferred on Syed Golam Hossin Khan. Rohtas Hill and the small plateau on which it is situated came to be Government Khas Mahal after the Mutiny. Raja Saho Mal's heirs gave back to the Company the grant made to the Raja in reward of his services. *Tilothu* was granted to the heirs of the Raja, the last *Killadar*. Chainpur and Sassaram and other portions were thus divested from the *Killadar's* territory.

During the reign of Akbar, Shahabad was comprised within Sarkar Rohtas, Todar Mal then fixed the revenue of Rohtas in 1582. The next settlement was effected in 1658 by Shuja Khan, when Rohtas was separated from Shahabad Bhojpur. In 1760 came on Aliverdy Khan's settlement. Mahomed Reja Khan altered the assessment in 1765, which was followed by the Permanent Settlement in 1793. The Fort was madeover to the East India Company by Raja Saho Mal as mentioned above. The Raja or his successor imposed a *sair* on all wood, bamboos or other forest produce. This right to levy a *sair* constituted the *Banskati Mahal.* This *Mahal* was originally conterminous with the Rohtas Parganah. Gradually the *Mahal* contracted by orders of withdrawal of the right in various parts. The *Banskati Mahal* is an estate of an exceptional right in a permanently settled district as Government does not possess any proprietory right in the land but only incorporeal rights on certain spontaneous products. The levy of *sair* is in the hands of a *Teshildar* of the *Banskati Mahal.* This *sair* and other dues are for the privilege of pasturage, working limekilns, collecting the produce of the forest, and for collecting cocoons, bark and cutting wood and bamboo &c and are of primitive origin and great antiquity.

□□□

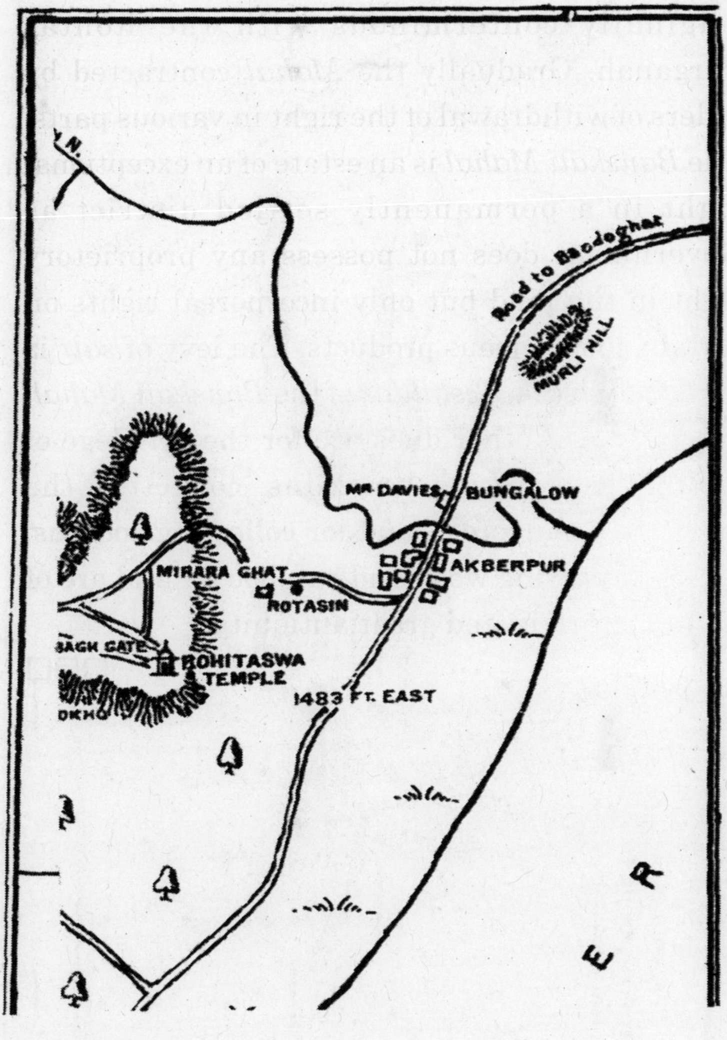
Road to Badoghat
MURLI HILL
MR. DAVIES
BUNGALOW
AKBERPUR
MIRARA GHAT
ROTASIN
ROHITASWA
TEMPLE
1483 FT. EAST

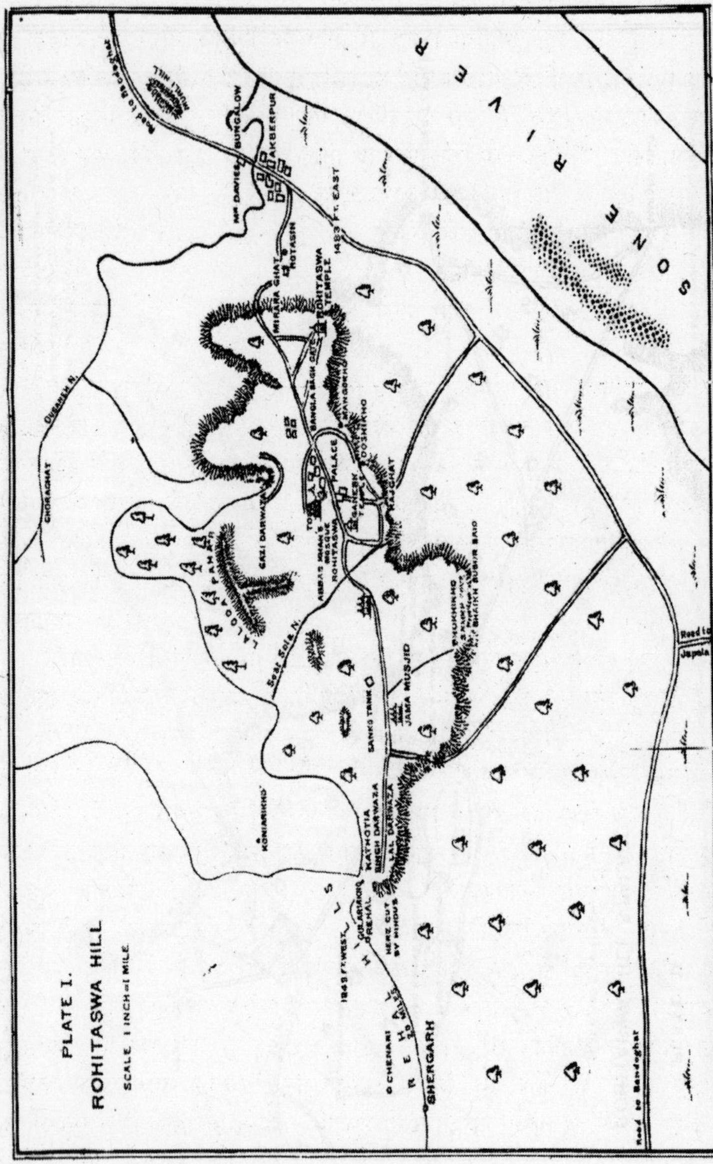
PLATE I.
ROHITASWA HILL
SCALE 1 INCH = 1 MILE
SHERGARH
JAMA MUSJID
SANKG TANK
PALACE
AKBERPUR
MIRARA GHAT
ROHITASWA TEMPLE
KATHOTIA
LAL DARWAZA
GAZI DARWAZA
SONE RIVER
Road to Bandoghat
Road to Japala

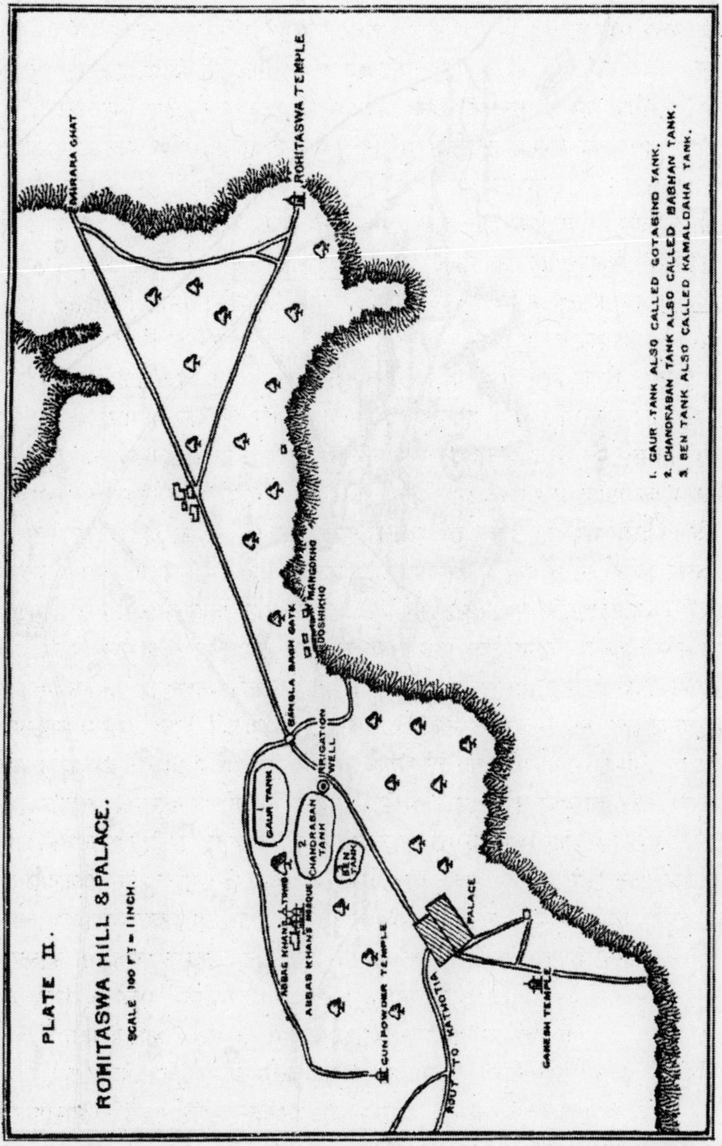
PLATE II.
ROHITASWA HILL & PALACE.
SCALE 100 FT = 1 INCH.
MIRARA GHAT
ROHITASWA TEMPLE
GAUR TANK
CHANDRABAN TANK
BEN TANK
IRRIGATION WELL
PALACE
GANESH TEMPLE
GUNPOWDER TEMPLE
ABBAS KHAN'S MOSQUE
1. GAUR TANK ALSO CALLED GOTABIND TANK.
2. CHANDRABAN TANK ALSO CALLED BABHAN TANK.
3. BEN TANK ALSO CALLED KAMALDAHA TANK.

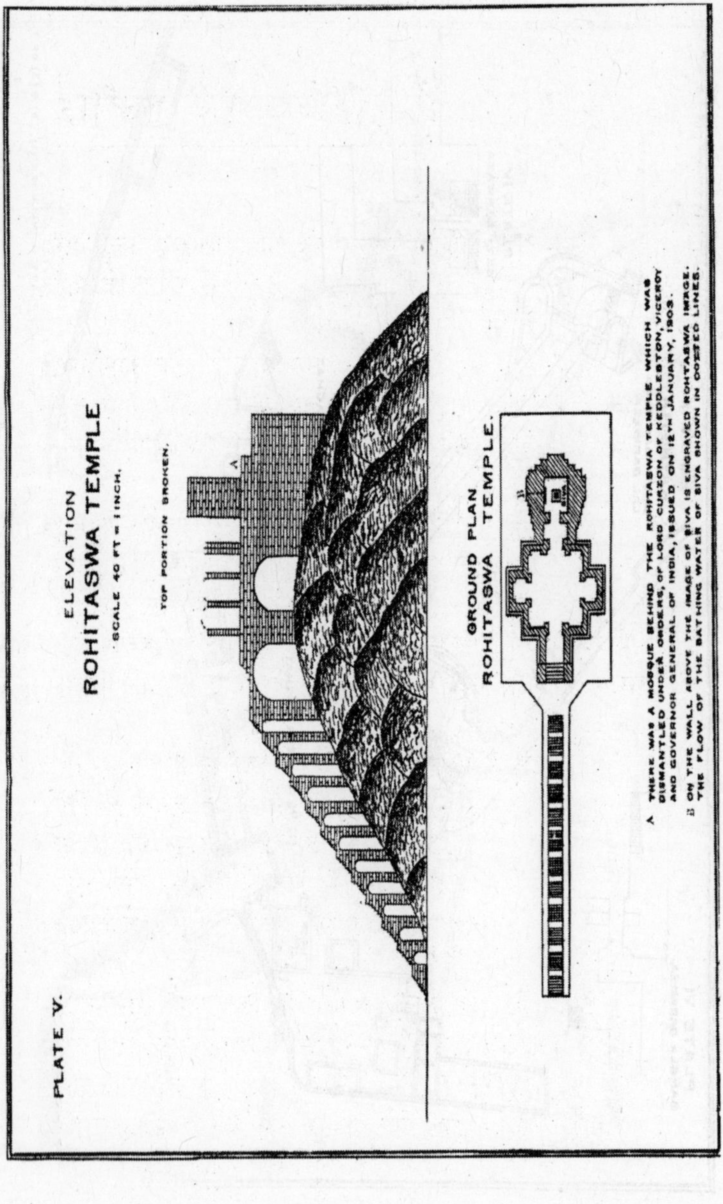
PLATE V.
ELEVATION
ROHITASWA TEMPLE
SCALE 40 FT = 1 INCH.
TOP PORTION BROKEN.
A
GROUND PLAN
ROHITASWA TEMPLE.
B
A THERE WAS A MOSQUE BEHIND THE ROHITASWA TEMPLE WHICH WAS DISMANTLED UNDER ORDERS, OF LORD CURZON OF KEDDLESTON, VICEROY AND GOVERNOR GENERAL OF INDIA, ISSUED ON 12TH JANUARY, 1903.
B ON THE WALL ABOVE THE IMAGE OF SIVA IS ENGRAVED ROHITASWA IMAGE. THE FLOW OF THE BATHING WATER OF SIVA SHOWN IN DOTTED LINES.

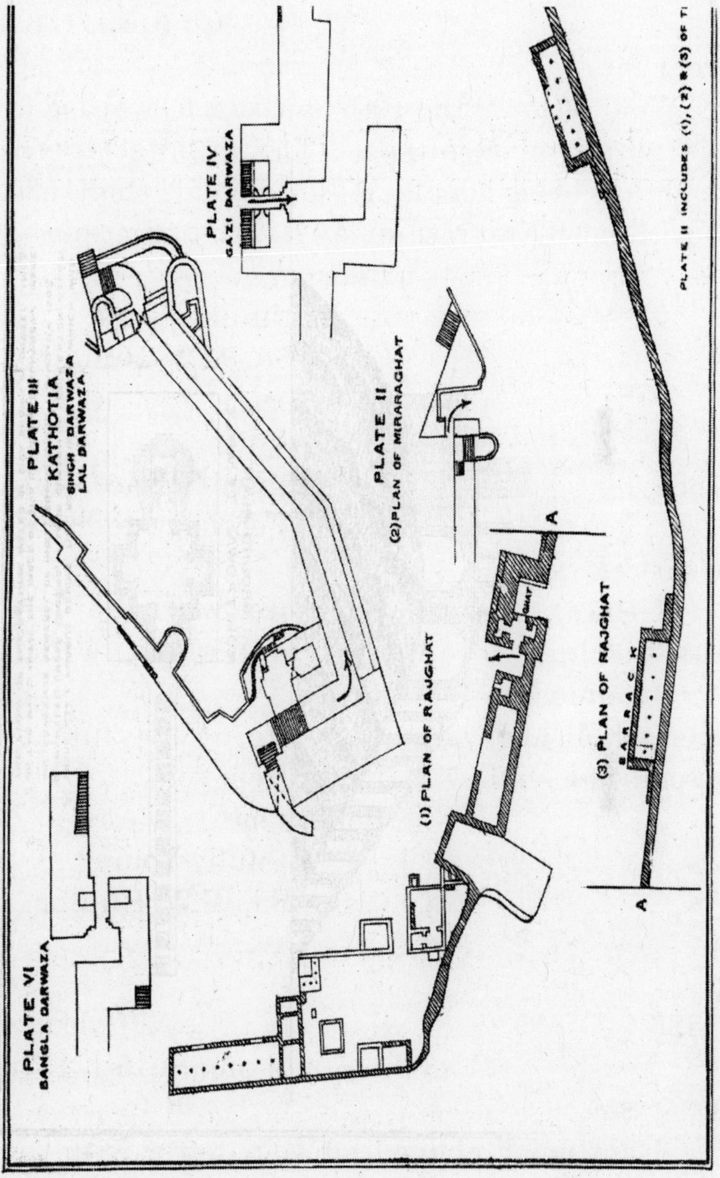
PLATE VI
BANGLA DARWAZA
PLATE III
KATHOTIA
SINGH DARWAZA
LAL DARWAZA
PLATE IV
GAZI DARWAZA
PLATE II
(2) PLAN OF MIRARAGHAT
(1) PLAN OF RAJGHAT
GHAT
A
A
(3) PLAN OF RAJGHAT
BARRACK
PLATE II INCLUDES (1), (2) & (3) OF

1884 Shimla

24th April, 1884

Dear Sir,

Your letter of the 19th has been forwarded to me while on a journey. The manuscript is doubtless being kept for me at Shimla. I shall read it with much interest on my return to that place.

I am,

Faithfully Yours,

Sd. W.W. Hunter

1885 United Service Club,

February 2nd 1885

Dear Sir,

I thank you for your note, with the very interesting account of Dahapara which accompanied it.

I shall always be happy to receive further papers of a similar character from you.

Believe me,

Faithfully Yours,

Sd. W.W. Hunter

1886 Calcutta

January 18th 1886

Dear Sir

I am much obliged for your letter with the account of Budh Gaya which accompanied it.

I have read your manuscript with interest, and have sent it to my office at Shimla to be filed with other papers for the new edition of the statistical account of the District, when it is called for.

Allow me to enclose a letter which I have lately received from Mr. Edwin Arnold, the author of the Light of *Asia*, on the subject.

If you care for Mr. Arnold's letter, please retain it.

It always gives me pleasure to hear from you and to find that a native gentleman has so genuine a talent for local research.

I am,

Very Faithfully Yours,

Sd. W.W. Hunter

Have you a copy of the pedigree of Nanda Kumar Roy who was hung for forgery in the time of Warren Hastings.

February 15th 1886

Dear Sir,

I am much obliged for your letter of the 13th with the pedigree of Raja Nanda Kumar.

* * * *

I am,

Faithfully Yours,

Sd. W.W. Hunter

I have much pleasure in certifying that Babu Wopendranath Ghosh has supplied me with valuable local materials regarding the families of Bishenpur, and Bangadhikari in the Murshidabad District.

U.S. Club Sd. W.W. Hunter
January 1st 1886 Director-General of Statistics

U. S. Club, Calcutta,
4th February 1886

Dear Sir,

I am much obliged to you for your letter of the 2nd February and for the paper on Gaya which it enclosed.

I am, Dear Sir,
Yours Faithfully,
Sd. W. W. Hunter.

Shimla, 9th August 1886

Dear Sir,

I am obliged for your letter of the 6th forwarding a Copy of your *Critical Notes on Wordsworth's Select Poems*. The little work seems a very meritorious one, and I should be happy to see you obtain promotion in your profession. But I do not think it would serve your purpose if I were to write formally to Mr. Croft at present. I hope to have an opportunity of seeing that gentleman in Calcutta before long.

I am,
Faithfully Yours,
Sd. W. W. Hunter

1888

Babu Wopendranath Ghosh, B.A.

Sir,

Thanks for your little book containing solutions of exercises on Geometrical conics.

Any book tending to lead F.A. Students beyond the study of mere book work in Conics, is deserving of success; and I think your work contains a good selection of exercises. Might I suggest that the next edition, an appendix of very easy problems without solution would be an improvement?

Yours truly,
Sd. J.H. Gilliland
Presidency College,
1st December 1888

1891

(From W. Fiddian Esq., M.A., C.S., Magistrate and Covenanted Deputy Collector of Howrah)

In the census department he has been of the

greatest service, especially in the abstraction and tabulation of the census figures, which have been under his sole charge, not only for this District but for a considerable part of the Burdwan census, which was handed over to this office at the last moment.

Report on the Census of the District of Howrah, 1891.

(The report was drafted entirely under the supervision of Mr. Fiddian from whom Mr. Grierson took charge shortly before its submission).

The following report on occupation by Babu Wopendranath Ghosh, Sub-Deputy Collector, Howrah.

(*Vide* letter No. 314 C dated the 21st December 1892 from G. A. Grierson, Esq., Magistrate of Howrah).

Special additional work of the district of Burdwan.—On the 24th June 1891 a quarter million population of 1314 blocks of *thanas Kaksa.* Kutugram, and Ranigang, of the district of Burdwan, was made over to this office for abstraction and tabulation. The abstraction of these *thanas* was begun just when the abstraction of Howrah was completed, and the tabulation was done simultaneously with the Howrah work which all was finished on the 4th September last. The second instalment of work received from Burdwan on the 24th September, 1891 was sent for tabulation only in registers I to XX, excepting the registers XVI and XVII of the following *thanas*, consisting of 2654 blocks, viz., *thanas* Satgach, Ausgram, Boodbud, Mon-golekote, Assensole and the Municipality of Raniganj. This work was commenced on the 28th of September with four gangs of tabulators. Another gang was added to the number in the second week, by whom the whole was completed. The office remained closed from the 8th to 18th on account of Durga Puja, during when all the tabulators were discharged. A third instalment of work received from the Magistrate of Burdwan, under the instructions of the Census Superintendent, on the 9th November 1891 for tabulation in registers XIV, XV, XIX and XX with totalling forms, consisted about 4000 blocks of the following *thanas*, viz., *thanas* Kaksa, Khandakosh, Monteswar, Jamalpur, Purbasthali, Burdwan, Shahebganj, Raona and the Municipalities of Kalna, Dainhat, Mankar, Burdwan and Katwa, This work was begun on the 13th November, and was completed on the 13th December when this office was finally closed. In these cases full task was turned out by most tabulators.

Inspection of Naogaon March 19th, 1893 by his Honour the Lieutenant-Governor of Bengal.

Para 11. Babu Wopendranath Ghosh is in-charge of the *Ganja* business, and though he has only been here for a short time, he seems to understand it well. He had prepared some interesting statistics for me some of which I utilise in this note.

1895

1 D.O. from Office of the Commissioner of Excise, Bengal.

Dear Wopendra Babu, I shall be glad to have a copy of your note on *ganja*. The Commissioner: may induce the Board to have it printed.

From Surgeon Captain D. Prain I.M.S., Curator of the Herbarium, Royal Botanical Garden, Sibpur, the 21st June, 1893.

1902

A manual for the guidance of the Revenue Division of the Sone Canals.

In conducting the enquiry into the manufacture of *ganja*, I have received the greatest assistance from the officers-in-charge of the Ganja Mahals at Naogaon, more especially from Babu

Wopendranath Ghosh, Sub-Deputy Collector there.

This manual which was drafted by Babu Wopendranath Ghosh, Deputy Collector, Sone canals Revenue Division, contains the procedure followed in the different branches of the Revenue Division Sone canals. It is designed for the guidance of the staff both of the Head Office and of the Moffusil collecting establishment.

Arrah J.H. Toowgood,
14th April, 1902 Supdg. Engineer

1906

This manual, drafted and revised by Babu Wopendranath Ghosh, Deputy Collector, Sone canals Revenue Division, contains procedure followed in the different branches of the Revenue Division of the Sone canals. It is designed for the guidance of the staff both of the Head Office and of the Moffusil collecting establishment.

Arrah J.H. Toowgood,
17th December 1906 Supdg. Engineer

From Secretary to the Chief Justice, Bengal, Sir Francis William Maclean, M.A. Kt., K.C.I.E.

"I am directed by the Chief Justice to convey

to you his best thanks for the Copy of your work on the, Land Acquisition Acts, which you have been good enough to send him and to say that His Lordship has no doubt but that it will prove a useful publication."

□□□